CHARLES SCHULZ

Gloria D. Miklowitz

ꝏ Dominie Press, Inc.

Publisher: Raymond Yuen
Editor: John S. F. Graham
Designer: Greg DiGenti
Photo Credits: Bettmann/Corbis (Page 6);
  D. Kirkland/Corbis (cover and Page 13); Reuters
  NewMedia Inc./Corbis (Page 20); AFP/Corbis
  (Page 27)

Published by:

℗ Dominie Press, Inc.
1949 Kellogg Avenue
Carlsbad, California 92008 USA

www.dominie.com

Paperback ISBN 0-7685-1216-6
Library Bound Edition ISBN 0-7685-1541-6
Printed in Singapore by PH Productions Pte Ltd
    4 5 6   09 08 07

Table of Contents

Chapter 1

Sparky

If you read the comics, you probably know and love "Peanuts." There's Charlie Brown, Lucy, Snoopy the beagle, Linus with his security blanket, the little red-haired girl, and others. They were all created by Charles "Sparky" Schulz, a shy man who began drawing cartoons as a child.

When Charles was in kindergarten, he drew a man shoveling snow in a storm with a palm tree in the scene. His teacher said, "Someday, Charles, you're going to be an artist."

Today, Charles' "Peanuts" comic appears in thousands of newspapers

Charles Schulz at his drawing table with sketches for "Peanuts"

throughout the country. "Peanuts" is considered the most successful comic strip in newspaper history.

He was born in 1922 to Dena and Carl Schulz of St. Paul, Minnesota. He was nicknamed "Sparky" when he was two days old. The name came from a horse named "Sparkplug" that appeared in a comic strip called "Barney Google."

From his early childhood, one of his greatest pleasures was to read the comics with his father, a barber. Charles bought all the comic books he could find and drew Buck Rogers, Popeye, Disney characters, and others in his notebooks.

His childhood was happy, with a loving, stable family. He enjoyed playing hockey and ball with his friends. He skipped two grades in elementary school and was the smallest and youngest in his sixth-grade class. Then he reached junior high and high school and failed almost everything.

In high school, he believed he was stupid and dreaded being called on in class. Still, he graduated on time, spending his spare time cartooning at the dining room table. He filled scrapbooks with his drawings of Sherlock Holmes, the famous storybook detective. He submitted some of his artwork to the high school yearbook, but it was rejected.

One evening his mother saw an ad in the paper which read: "Do you like to draw? Send for our free talent test." The course cost $170, a lot of money in those days. But his father paid for it. Charles took the lessons by mail, while he was working. He made $16 a week at one of his jobs, and it gave him a chance to draw. But it was 1943, and America was at war. Charles was drafted into the U.S. Army.

Chapter 2

Check Tuesday
for Spot Drawing

When Charles entered the Army in 1943, his mother, who had encouraged his drawing, was dying of cancer. One Sunday evening, on leave to visit her, his mother said, "I suppose we should say goodbye because we probably will never see each other again." She died the next day. Her loss made Charles very sad and lonely, feelings he later gave to Charlie Brown.

Much of his time in the army was spent in Europe. He served in Germany, France, and Austria in the last years of World War II.

When he returned from the war, he looked for work in art departments near home, but no one wanted him. He took samples of his work to *Topix*, a comic-book style Catholic magazine. The art director did not buy his cartoons, but gave him lettering to do on the panels of comic strips that other artists had drawn.

Charles would get up early, deliver his lettering work, then go to teach at the art school where he had once studied. In the evening, he would letter other people's comic drawings, often working until midnight. Soon he was drawing the words for comics in French and Spanish, even though he didn't know what the words meant.

Charles came up with the idea of using tiny kids as subjects for cartoons. The first of these cartoons ran in *Topix*. He signed these cartoons, "By Sparky." A friend suggested he show samples of his "kids" to the St. Paul Pioneer Press newspaper. He did, calling the panels "Li'l Folks." The paper ran it once a week for two years.

During this time, he was also drawing and sending different cartoons to magazines, in hopes of selling them, but without much luck. The first

Charles Schulz poses in front of a stained glass window featuring his "Peanuts" characters

13

acceptance came from *The Saturday Evening Post*. The letter read, "Check Tuesday for spot drawing of boy on lounge." He thought that meant his drawing was being returned, but instead it meant they were buying it! He sold 15 cartoons to that magazine between 1948 and 1950.

Chapter 3

A Lot of His Own Life

In 1950, Charles Schulz sent samples of his work to United Feature Syndicate in New York. A syndicate can sell an artist or writer's work to many newspapers at once, saving work and time. After weeks of not hearing anything, Charles wrote again. Finally, the editorial director answered, inviting him to New York to talk about his work.

Charles arrived at United Feature Syndicate's office early one morning, before the director arrived. He left drawings of a new comic strip he'd been working on and went to breakfast. When he returned to the office, he found the staff excited about the drawings. They offered him a contract for five years, but they wanted to change the name from "Li'l Folks" to "Peanuts." Charles never liked the name. He said it was confusing and undignified. He said that no one ever called small children "peanuts." But he agreed to the change.

The strip appeared for the first time on October 2, 1950, in nine newspapers. By the end of the first year, 35 newspapers were carrying it. The next year, that number increased to 45. More newspapers started carrying it each year.

Only four characters appeared in the first strip: Charlie Brown, Snoopy, Sherm, and Patty. In future years, the cast increased to Schroeder, Lucy, Linus, Sally (Charlie Brown's sister), Frieda, Franklin, Woodstock, Pigpen, and Marcie.

With a steady income, Charles bought a new car, the first he had ever owned. He also proposed marriage to a red-haired girl he was in love with and dating at the time, but she married someone else. In his comic strip, Charlie Brown is always trying to get the "little red-haired girl" to like him. He put a lot of his own life into his comic strip.

Charles always worked six weeks ahead of deadline, doing his own drawing, inking, lettering, and storylines. Imagine having to come up with a new idea every day of the year for 50 years!

Despite his success, Charles often felt depressed and fearful of change. He said he was a worrier, and so Charlie Brown was a worrier, too.

Chapter 4

An Active Imagination

"Peanuts" touches people because Charles Schulz wrote from his own life and feelings. He believed that happiness was about simple things, like supper, a soaring kite, or jumping in a pile of leaves. "Happiness is a warm puppy," he wrote.

Still, he saw himself as the boy
whose artwork was rejected for the high
school yearbook and as the boy who
was rejected by the little red-haired girl.
"I was a bland, stupid-looking kid

Charles Schulz celebrates his career with a star on the Hollywood Walk of Fame

who started off badly and failed at everything," he once told a reporter.

Snoopy was based on his childhood dog, Spike. At first, Snoopy was just a cute beagle, but by the 1960s, the dog's thoughts were shown in thought balloons over his head. It gave Charles many possibilities.

Snoopy had an active imagination. He was the World War I flying ace, flying an imaginary airplane—a Sopwith Camel—against the Red Baron. He was the author of great adventure and romance novels. He was also Joe Cool, who hung out in sunglasses and snapped his fingers.

Through the years, we came to know everything that is in Snoopy's doghouse: a pool table, a Ping-Pong table, bunk beds, a Van Gogh painting, and a whirlpool.

One of Charles's most famous cartoons was to commemorate D-Day, the day Allied forces landed in Normandy, France during World War II. It showed Snoopy as a soldier with a helmet making his way from the surf to the shore.

In 1951, Charles married Joyce Halverson. They moved to Santa Rosa, California, where they raised five children in a house he and his wife designed. They divorced in 1972.

Charles got some of his ideas for the comic strip from his own children. He saw his children drag their blankets around the house, and so he drew Linus with a security blanket that he dragged around everywhere.

In 1965, "Peanuts" was made into a television special, "A Charlie Brown Christmas." It became a holiday classic, with jazz music and children's voices.

"Peanuts" has been featured in more than 50 TV specials, four feature films, more than 1,400 books and countless products. There is even a Broadway musical, *You're a Good Man, Charlie Brown*.

Chapter 5

The Shy Man Who Loved to Draw Cartoons

A highlight in Charles Schulz's life came when Apollo 10 was launched. NASA named the command module *Charlie Brown* and the lunar module *Snoopy*. Charles said there was "never a beagle who flew a Sopwith Camel one day and a spacecraft the next!"

The worldwide success of "Peanuts" brought fame and wealth to the shy man who loved to draw cartoons as a child. Forbes magazine estimated that Charles earned $33 million in 1996. But the man everyone called "Sparky" lived a simple life. He owned an ice-skating rink in Santa Rosa, where he skated almost every day. He played in an ice-hockey league with friends. It was there that he met Jeannie Forsyth, who he married. A simple man, he didn't like to travel, but enjoyed his family, home, reading, and work.

In 1998, the Schulzes donated $5 million to a new library at Sonoma State University, his wife's college. They often wrote checks to friends in need without being asked.

Worsening health forced Charles to

retire in 1999. He could no longer draw his comic strip. He said retirement would give him more time to focus on his health and family without the worry of a daily deadline.

He died of cancer on February 12, 2000, at age 77. Condolences came in from all over the world. He had touched millions of people's lives by writing about and drawing kids who never grew up.

Charles Schulz after being honored by the
French Ministry of Culture in Paris

Glossary

Acceptance - when a publisher agrees to publish material.

Allied forces - in World War II, the Allies included the United States, England, France, Russia, Australia, and Canada. Forces from the Allies fought against the Axis powers—Germany, Italy, and Japan.

Apollo - the United States' space project that sent spaceships to the moon.

Austria - a small country in central Europe.

Beagle - an intelligent small dog with big floppy ears.

Broadway - a street in New York famous for theater productions.

Catholic - a religion. The Pope is the leader of the Catholic Church.

Commemorate - to honor a certain day or event in history, usually on the same date.

Contract - a legal agreement between two people or groups that states what each will do for the other.

Deadline - in publishing, the time when artwork or a manuscript is due to be able to print it on time.

D-Day - in World War II, Germany had defeated France. The United States, Canada, and England planned together to invade France on June 6, 1944, to push the Germans out. The plan eventually succeeded, but many people were killed.

Detective - someone who solves crimes by following clues.

Dreaded - thought something bad would happen.

Inking - when an artist makes sketches in pencil and then draws over the best lines in pen and ink.

Jazz - a type of music where the players make the music up as they go along.

Lettering - in a comic strip, the words that appear alongside the pictures, often as speech from the characters. Sometimes one person draws the pictures for a comic strip, and another person "letters" it.

Li'l - a contraction of "little" (slang).

Lunar - having to do with the moon.

Module - a separate part of a rocket or spacecraft that can separate from the main part.

NASA - the government agency that makes and launches rockets and shuttles that go into space.

Normandy - a region in France. The invasion of France on D-day happened here. see *D-Day*

Panel - a scene in a comic strip. Some comic strips have only one panel, others can have up to four or five—sometimes twelve on Sundays.

Popeye - a cartoon character from the 1920s and 1930s.

Red Baron - In World War I, Baron von Richthofen was an expert pilot who flew a red triplane (an airplane with three sets of wings) for Germany. American and British pilots called him the Red Baron because of the color of his plane.

Santa Rosa - a small city north of San Francisco, California.

Sherlock Holmes - a fictional detective in a series of mystery books written by Sir Arthur Conan Doyle.

Sonoma - a small city north of San Francisco, California.

Sopwith Camel - a biplane (an airplane with two sets of wings) that British and Canadian pilots flew against Germany during World War I. The Sopwith Aviation Company made a number of biplanes and triplanes in World War I.

Submitted - when a writer or artist sends a manuscript or cartoon somewhere to be reviewed by publishers. If the publishers like it, they can pay for it and print it.

Syndicate - an organization that sells the work of someone to more than one company.

Undignified - not something to be proud of.

Van Gogh - Vincent Van Gogh, a Dutch painter in the 1800s. His artwork is considered to be very valuable.

Whirlpool - a type of bathtub that uses jets to swirl water and air bubbles around.